VALUES

Responsibility

Kimberley Jane Pryor

MACMILLAN LIBRARY

First published in 2010 by
MACMILLAN EDUCATION AUSTRALIA PTY LTD
15–19 Claremont Street, South Yarra 3141

Visit our website at www.macmillan.com.au or go directly
to http://www.macmillanlibrary.com.au

Associated companies and representatives throughout the world.

Copyright © Kimberley Jane Pryor 2010

All rights reserved.
Except under the conditions described in the *Copyright Act 1968* of Australia
and subsequent amendments, no part of this publication may be reproduced,
stored in a retrieval system, or transmitted in any form or by any means,
electronic, mechanical, photocopying, recording or otherwise, without the
prior written permission of the copyright owner.

Educational institutions copying any part of this book for educational purposes
under the Act must be covered by a Copyright Agency Limited (CAL) licence
for educational institutions and must have given a remuneration notice to CAL.
Licence restrictions must be adhered to. Any copies must be photocopies only,
and they must not be hired out or sold. For details of the CAL licence contact:
Copyright Agency Limited, Level 15, 233 Castlereagh Street, Sydney, NSW 2000.
Telephone: (02) 9394 7600. Facsimile: (02) 9394 7601. Email: info@copyright.com.au

National Library of Australia Cataloguing-in-Publication entry

Pryor, Kimberley Jane, 1962–
    Responsibility / Kimberley Jane Pryor.
    ISBN: 9781420278248 (hbk.)
    Pryor, Kimberley Jane, 1962– Values.
    Includes index.
    For primary school age.
    Responsibility—Juvenile literature.
179.9

Managing Editor: Vanessa Lanaway
Editor: Helena Newton
Proofreader: Kirstie Innes-Will
Designer: Kerri Wilson
Page layout: Pier Vido
Photo researcher: Sarah Johnson (management: Debbie Gallagher)
Production Controller: Vanessa Johnson

Printed in China

Acknowledgements
The author and the publisher are grateful to the following for permission to reproduce copyright material:

Front cover photograph: Young boy watching dog eat, Chris Amaral/Getty Images

Photos courtesy of:
Chris Amaral/Getty Images, **1**, **6**; Alistair Berg/Getty Images, **9**; John Churchman/Getty Images, **4**; Tanya Constantine/Getty Images, **22**; Adam Crowley/Getty Images, **30**; David Deas/Getty Images, **29**; Jack Hollingsworth/Getty Images, **25**; Image Source/Getty Images, **18**; Deborah Jaffe/Getty Images, **15**; Jupiterimages/Getty Images, **19**; Eri Morita/Getty Images, **26**; Lori Adamski Peek/Getty Images, **26**; redcover.com/Getty Images, **17**; Don Smetzer/Getty Images, **13**; Somos/Veer/Getty Images, **14**; Jupiter Unlimited, **23**; BrandX Pictures/Photolibrary, **12**; Corbis/Photolibrary, **7**; Corbis/Photolibrary, **10**; Richard Hutchings/Photolibrary, **24**; Lawrence Migdale/Photolibrary, **11**; Photo Researchers/Photolibrary, **27**; Tomas Rodriguez/Photolibrary, **5**; Busse Yankushev/Photolibrary, **8**; © Jaimie Duplass/Shutterstock, **21**; Stockxpert, **3**, **16**, **20**.

While every care has been taken to trace and acknowledge copyright, the publisher tenders their apologies for any accidental infringement where copyright has proved untraceable. Where the attempt has been unsuccessful, the publisher welcomes information that would redress the situation.

For Nick, Ashley and Thomas

Contents

Values	4
Responsibility	6
Responsible people	8
Showing responsibility with family	10
Showing responsibility with friends	12
Showing responsibility with neighbours	14
Ways to show responsibility	16
Thinking before you act	18
Keeping promises	20
Doing what you are supposed to	22
Fixing mistakes	24
Helping your community	26
Protecting the environment	28
Personal set of values	30
Glossary	31
Index	32

When a word is printed in **bold**, you can look up its meaning in the Glossary on page 31.

Values

Values are the things you believe in. They guide the way:
- you think
- you speak
- you **behave**.

Values help you to behave safely while watching fireworks.

Values help you to decide what is right and what is wrong. They also help you to live your life in a meaningful way.

Values help you to follow the rules when playing a game such as leapfrog.

Responsibility

Responsibility is doing what needs to be done. It is doing a job as well as you can, and at the right time.

It is responsible to feed your dog the right food at regular mealtimes.

Responsibility is also thinking before you act. It is **considering** the effect your actions will have on yourself, others and the environment.

You might wake people up if you practise playing your drums early in the morning.

Responsible people

Responsible people are **accountable** for their actions. They do not make **excuses** or blame others when things go wrong. They try to learn from their mistakes.

People who find rust on their bicycles learn to keep their bicycles clean and dry.

Responsible people are **reliable**. They keep promises to their family, friends and neighbours.

Responsible people can be relied on to pack sports equipment away.

Showing responsibility with family

Family members show responsibility by doing jobs around the home without being asked. They know it takes **effort** and teamwork to keep a home clean and tidy.

Laundry can be folded more quickly when family members work together.

Responsible people take good care of family pets. They give their pets enough food and water. They also keep their pets clean, and spend time with them.

Brushing your horse after riding is a responsible thing to do.

Showing responsibility with friends

Responsible people make good decisions when they are with their friends. They do what is right instead of what is easy.

Putting on protective clothing to go skateboarding with a friend shows responsibility.

Responsible people make friends with people with extra needs. They invite them to join their groups. They also introduce them to their other friends.

You can have a lot of fun with a friend with extra needs.

Showing responsibility with neighbours

Neighbours show responsibility by helping each other. A neighbour who is sick or hurt may need help with jobs around the home. A lonely neighbour may need someone to talk to.

Remembering to check a sick neighbour's letterbox shows responsibility.

Neighbours also show responsibility by following the rules in their neighbourhood. They know that the rules are there to keep them safe and protect their **rights**.

Responsible people wait outside a closed pool gate until an adult opens it.

Ways to show responsibility

There are many different ways to show responsibility with your family, friends and neighbours. Thinking before you act is a good way to start being responsible.

Responsible people think about which food is healthiest before choosing a snack.

Keeping promises and doing what you are supposed to are good ways to show responsibility. Fixing mistakes is another way to show responsibility.

Packing your toys away when you have finished playing shows responsibility.

Thinking before you act

Thinking before you act is one way to show responsibility. Responsible people think about what might happen if they decide to do something.

You might break something if you decide to run in a shop.

Responsible people also think about what might happen if they decide not to do something. Some jobs need to be done so others do not miss out or get hurt.

Other people might trip over your toys if you decide not to pick them up.

Keeping promises

Keeping promises is another way to show responsibility. Responsible people keep their promises because they do not like to let others down.

Keeping your promise to walk home with a younger family member shows responsibility.

Responsible people make promises and plan to keep them. They only promise to do things they have time for. They tell others if they realise they cannot keep a promise.

A friend may feel worried or annoyed if you break your promise to meet her.

Doing what you are supposed to

Doing what you are supposed to also shows responsibility. Responsible people make sure that they do their homework. They also give it to their teacher on time.

Teachers find it easier to mark homework that is handed in on time.

Responsible people also go to lessons at the right time. They remember to take the equipment they need. They do not expect other people to remind them.

Responsible students take their martial arts uniform to lessons every week.

Fixing mistakes

Fixing mistakes is a good way to be responsible. When responsible people make messes, they clean them up. They do not leave them for other people to clean up.

Cleaning up spilled paint as soon as possible is one way to be responsible.

Responsible people ask others for help if they make mistakes. They also offer to help other people fix their mistakes.

An older family member may be able to help you fix a broken remote-control car.

Helping your community

Helping your **community** is another way to be responsible. Each person has something to offer their community. Younger people have ideas and energy, and older people have **knowledge** and **skills**.

Younger people sometimes help their community by planting trees.

Responsible people take part in community activities and help to make community decisions. They also help to keep their neighbourhood clean.

Responsible people sometimes pick up rubbish around local waterways.

Protecting the environment

Protecting the environment is a responsible thing to do. Reducing pollution is one way to protect the environment. Using the car less reduces pollution because cars cause pollution.

Walking instead of travelling in a car for short trips helps protect the environment.

Reducing waste is another way to protect the environment. Recycling reduces waste because it changes used products into new products.

Plastic bottles can be put into special bins for recycling.

Personal set of values

There are many different values. Everyone has a personal set of values. This set of values guides people in big and little ways in their daily lives.

Lifeguards are responsible for keeping people safe at beaches.

Glossary

accountable   able to explain what you have done

behave   act in a certain way

community   people who live near each other and help each other

considering   thinking about

effort   hard work

excuses   reasons why things have not been done properly

knowledge   things you know and understand

reliable   able to be relied or depended on

rights   things that everyone should be allowed to do or have, such as the right to go to school

skills   abilities that help you to do activities or jobs well

Index

a
accountability 8
actions 7, 8

b
blaming 8

c
community 26–27

d
decisions 5, 12, 18–19, 27

e
effort 10
environment 7, 28–29
equipment 9, 23
excuses 8

f
families 9, 10–11, 16, 20, 25
friends 9, 12–13, 16, 21

i
ideas 26

k
knowledge 26

m
mistakes 8, 17, 24–25

n
neighbours 9, 14–15, 16

p
pets 6, 11
pollution 28
promises 9, 17, 20–21

r
recycling 29
reliability 9
rights 15
rules 5, 15

s
skills 26

t
teamwork 10
thinking 4, 7, 16, 18–19

v
values 4–5, 30

w
waste 29